Roadside Picnic
Revisited
Seven Articles on the
Soviet Novel That
Inspired the Film
Stalker

MICHAEL ANDRE-DRIUSSI

ISBN: 1947614002
ISBN-13: 9781947614000

"A *Roadside Picnic* Triptych" originally appeared in *The New York Review of Science Fiction No. 281*, January 2012.

"Notes on the New Translation of *Roadside Picnic*" originally appeared in *The New York Review of Science Fiction No. 286*, June 2012.

"The Politics of *Roadside Picnic*" originally appeared in *The New York Review of Science Fiction No. 292*, December 2012.

"Stalky v. Stalker, or, *Stalky & Co.* against *Roadside Picnic*" originally appeared in *The New York Review of Science Fiction No. 327*, November 2015.

"The Lost Strugatsky Triptych: *Unintended Meetings*" originally appeared in *The New York Review of Science Fiction No. 323*, July 2015.

"Searching for the Worst Edition of *Roadside Picnic*" appears here for the first time, 2016.

"Review of *The Dead Mountaineer's Inn*" originally appeared in *The New York Review of Science Fiction No. 323*, July 2015.

CONTENTS

A *ROADSIDE PICNIC* TRIPTYCH

I. The "Magic Key" to *Roadside Picnic*

I recently read *Roadside Picnic* by Arkady and Boris Strugatsky (translated 1977), a Soviet sf novel that has been available in English translation for over 30 years, and upon rereading it some weeks later I discovered a magic key resolving a central problem that has baffled essayists for decades.

The main sticking point is the novel's ambiguous ending. Here are a number of quotes to show the reaction:

• We never learn whether or not the Golden Ball is capable of granting such a wish. —Stephen W. Potts, *The Second Marxian Invasion,* 1991 (80)

• That is the last line of the novel, so we are not sure whether his wish is granted. —Carl Darryl Malmgren, *Worlds Apart,* 1991 (117)

• We have no way of knowing whether the "wish machine" will grant his utopian plea or, for that matter, whether it might — in the tradition of fairy tales and of systems theory — grant the wish, only to accompany it with unexpected and terrible "side-effects." —Brooks Landon, *Science Fiction After 1900,* 2002 (104)

1

• Will this wish be realized, or is it a cruel joke, a futile wish … The very openness of the end may be understood as a glimpse of either utopia or dystopia. —Roland Boer, *Knockin' on Heaven's Door,* 1991 (121)

Here, then, is the magic key that I thought I had found: if a reader tracks the semi-hidden time clues within the text, the end of the book does not come at the chronological end at all — the introduction actually comes at that point, and it is nine years later.

Time Clues
• Section 0: Thirty years after the alien Visitation (4).
• Section 1: Red is twenty-three years old (41).
• Section 2: Red is twenty-eight, and he had been ten at the Visitation (57), so it is Year 18.
• Section 3: Red is just out of prison, and he served two years (117), so it is Year 20.
• Section 4: Red is thirty-one so it is Year 21.
(Page citations are from the Gollancz "SF Masterworks" edition, Orion, 2007)

•

Should a reader accept the introduction as an afterword, nearly all of the ambiguity is removed. Nine years have passed, and there is no "reality change" to the world or even any noteworthy change to the town where Red lived. Thus, there is definitely no utopian result, and there seems to be no evidence of a dystopian result, either — there is simply no change.

II. My Circling Path to *Roadside Picnic*
I saw the Soviet sf movie *Stalker,* based on *Roadside Picnic,* during its first American run in the early 1980s. Having seen a few Soviet sf movies (*Voyage to the Prehistoric Planet* [1965], *Solaris* [1972], and *To the Stars by Hard Ways* [1982]), I felt it was the best of them, but it was hardly a favorite,

so I was not inclined to read the book.

Stalker inspired a series of computer games. In 2011, I played the third one, *Call of Pripyat* (2010). It was good, especially in atmosphere as a sort of "survival horror" type of thing.

Finally, almost by accident, I read *Roadside Picnic* and found that, despite my secondary exposures, I had no real concept of it.

The novel's introduction is a radio interview of a famous scientist, exactly the sort of context-building one expects at the start of Soviet sf or Wellsian sf, yet in this case it is remarkably brief and sly, so that it seems to be a light-hearted, humorous take on stodgy convention. As a result, I suspected that the novel itself would be a comedy in the pattern of Stanislaw Lem, but in this regard I was completely misled.

Section One is told from the point of view of a man called Red. A former stalker or scavenger of alien artifacts, he has reformed his criminal ways and is now legally employed as a lab assistant at the Institute, but the scientist he works for has hit the limits in studying the typical alien artifacts he possesses. Red knows his boss needs something new, and he knows just where to find it in the Zone that exists next to town. Thus begins the story of their expedition, and the tension ratchets up masterfully as they approach the Zone and then as they pass through its various stages. The tone creates an intriguing fusion of opposites between the hard-boiled style and the creepy, spooky sort of Wonderland, of the Zone.

Section Two is set five years later and opens with Red hiding in the cemetery from a patrol. If the first adventure was mainly about entering the Zone as a sort of prospector, this second one is mainly about getting out and disposing of the artifacts. Told in the third person, now the criminal aspect of stalkers comes into sharp focus. The episode is a nail-biter, a pure rush of Dashiell Hammett caliber action, mystery, twist, and surprise.

Section Three seems to explode everything that had come before, since it shifts to follow a day in the life of a minor character, a bureaucrat who works for the Institute. It starts off in the light-hearted style of the Introduction, but as it progresses, it darkens as we see that this jovial bureaucrat is also a rising crime boss who owns a brothel. He has a mystery, and he also solves it, but in a way that is almost anti-mystery.

Section Four returns us to Red on a stalker mission deep in the Zone. At this stage, the extreme nature of the situation pushes the story into the dark and troubling realm of fairy tale as it grinds along to that baffling ending.

In short, I think that *Roadside Picnic* is top notch. It exploded my head the first time I read it, and did it again the second time, then once more on the third time. I love it for its variety of narration and its mash-up of different genres (sf, mystery, crime, fairy tale, comedy, adventure). It is like a Chinese puzzle box with all sorts of amazing bits within. I would say it is like Zelazny's *Jack of Shadows* (1971) where the daylight part of a tide-locked world is technological and normal but the dark side is a place of magic and "fantasy" — only here the dark tone is as close as the town and the Zone.

Many of the sections in *Roadside Picnic* have a "Cask of Amontillado" moment, a twist wherein the reader recoils in horror from the previously sympathetic character. This is obviously the case in Section Three with the bureaucrat who is revealed to be a brutal crime boss, but it happens regularly with Red.

The first case is the most mild. Red is a good guy in this world, and we understand that he has reformed to the point of taking on legitimate employment, so we are surprised to discover in Section One that he has continued moonlighting as a stalker. At the end of Section Two we are appalled to find that he has successfully smuggled a weapon of mass destruction out of the Zone. Near the conclusion of the novel he sacrifices a young man for his own goal, effectively becoming exactly the sort of crime boss he has despised for so long.

III. Stalking the Mirage

I kept bearing down on the text and it seemed to break at a few points; that is, it seemed to lie outright in order to create a surprise later. For example, there's a moment in Section One where Red is narrating the story directly to the reader and he says of a character, "He sure is a funny guy" (17) where, in hindsight, the verb should be "was," but this would telegraph his fate. So this would seem to be a literary dodge, an artifice to subliminally amplify a later effect. (The Russian original is ambiguous on this point.)

Another example comes a few pages earlier, when Red speaks to someone about some anomalous trucks out in the Zone: "They've been exposed to the elements for thirty years and they're just like new" (14). That span of 30 years echoes the 30-year anniversary mentioned in the introduction (4, 5), yet it cannot be correct since the year must be less than 20. It happens again one paragraph later: "Like everything was the way it was thirty years ago" (14). So it has to be a lie, to preserve the fiction that the introduction comes first. Right?

One must be thorough. While I cannot read Russian, I found online a side-by-side version of *Roadside Picnic* in Russian and English. I found the suspect lines in Russian and fed them into Google Translation:

- "thirtieth anniversary" (4): thirteenth
- "these thirty years" (5): thirteen
- "exposed for thirty years" (14): thirteen
- "way it was thirty years ago" (14): thirteen

In this manner I lost the magic key and discovered that my paperback's translation was faulty.

Then I wanted to find out when the error had crept in. I looked at many different editions (hardcopy Gollancz

2007; e-text Cryptomaoist Edition; e-text download from Russian sf page; and online parallel translation text), all the same, and finally the English first edition (published together with *Tale of the Troika* and an introduction by Theodore Sturgeon). It, too, has the errors. It seems as though the English translation had these errors from the start, and they have never been corrected.

Not one to miss the obvious, I went online and found a Russian who had a first edition Russian copy and I asked him about those passages. They checked out, so the error was not in the Russian online text I was using, it was in the English online text right next to it.

Where does this leave us?

The ambiguous ending has been restored.

Granted that, it seems to me that the three basic solutions are utopian, dystopian, and mundane. The first two are an apocalyptic pair: in the utopian ending, the Golden Ball grants Red's wish and reality itself is changed — which is why the text breaks off. The dystopian ending that I see is a worship of bloodthirsty Satanic gods, something out of the Book of Revelation. The mundane ending would look like my magic key ending in that the wish is not granted and Red's situation is the standard "human condition," aside from the fact that he just committed human sacrifice to an alien idol.

Because I see the story as being really about Red's downward spiral, a tale of the "anti-Job," I have difficulty in seeing the utopian outcome as being supported by the text in any way. The "holy grail" analogy used by Fredric Jameson in his 1982 article (collected in *Archaeologies of the Future,* 2005) gets a boost from the text because the sacrificed man is named "Arthur." It gives me a glimpse of the utopian reading by perhaps implying that Red, despite his murder of Arthur, is still the only good man in town and thus a kind of Galahad.

So when I stumble into the bar, bruised and battered from the Zone, stupid with fatigue, and a familiar voice calls out, "Hey, stalker," this is the tale I will tell: *the one that got away.*

****

Works Cited

Boer, Roland. *Knockin' on Heaven's Door.* London; New York: Routledge, 1991.

Jameson, Fredric. *Archaeologies of the Future.* London: Verso, 2007.

Landon, Brooks. *Science Fiction After 1900.* New York: Routledge, 2002.

Malmgren, Carl Darryl. *Worlds Apart: Narratology of Science Fiction.* Bloomington, Indiana: Indiana University Press, 1991.

Potts, Stephen W. *The Second Marxian Invasion.* San Bernardino, California: Borgo Press, 1991.

Strugatsky, Arkady and Boris. *Roadside Picnic,* translated by Antonina W. Bouis. Different editions as follows:

———. First edition. Omnibus with *Tale of the Troika.* New York: Macmillan, 1977.

———. Gollancz (S.F. Masterworks Edition). London: Orion, 2007.

———. E-text. Cryptomaoist Edition. PDF.

———. E-text. Download from Russian sf page. PDF.

———. Parallel Russian/English online text. <http://www.shnaresys.com/roadside/picnic/parallel.htm> Accessed August 29, 2011.

NOTES ON THE NEW TRANSLATION
OF *ROADSIDE PICNIC*

Roadside Picnic. Translated by Olena Bormashenko. Chicago: Chicago Review Press, 2012.

A new translation of the Soviet novel *Roadside Picnic* by Arkady and Boris Strugatsky recently came out. I am happy to report that, even though I had nothing to do with it, the vexing errors I found in the old edition (translated by Antonina W. Bouis, 1977) have all been repaired.

But wait — there's more! More text, that is! Because Bormashenko translated a manuscript that had not been censored by the Soviets. This is the novel as it was intended.

In reading this new translation, I found several cases of new passages within the text: one has to do with the location of another Zone; another has to do with Red's zombie father; a third involves details regarding the seductive bombshell Dina Burbridge; there is more about Red's mutant-daughter Monkey screaming at night; and finally, a part about roughing it in the Zone. I found these bits to be very interesting, opening up the text in new ways.

Details about another Zone

In Noonan's section of the novel, there is a part where he
is driving his car through town after he has been chewed
out by the general. He ponders his current situation in
comparison to a bad time he once had in Singapore:

> So what, I got my face slammed down on the table
> one lousy time! It could have been worse. It could
> have been some other part of me and it could have
> been something with nails in it instead of a table. All
> right, let's stay on the track. Where's my little
> establishment? (Bouis translation, 93)

Noonan's thoughts amount to a recognition that, while his
current position is bad, it isn't as bad as it was in
Singapore, and even that could have been worse.

In the new translation, Noonan expands upon this to
make mention of another Zone by name. This is very
interesting, because the old translation says that there are
six Zones (Bouis translation, 3), but only names the one in
(fictitious) Harmont, a mining town somewhere in Canada.
The Zones are said to lie on a "very smooth curve" (4), as
if they were shot onto the spinning globe from the star
Deneb (3).

> Big deal — your face got slammed against the table.
> It might have been worse. It might not have been
> your face, and it might not have been a table, but
> something nail studded … My God, this could all
> be so simple! We could round up these scum
> [stalkers] and put them away for a decade … or
> send them the hell away! Now, in Russia they've
> never even heard of stalkers. Over there, they really
> have an empty belt around the Zone — a hundred
> miles wide, with no one around, none of these
> stinking tourists, and no Burbridges. *Think simple,*
> *gentlemen! I swear this doesn't need to be so complicated. No*

business in the Zone — goodbye, off you go to the hundred and first mile. All right, let's not get sidetracked. Where's my little establishment? (Bormashenko translation, 120; ellipses in original).

This bit about a Russian Zone gives a second map point, and seems to confirm my earlier suspicion that all the Zones are along a line of latitude shared by Canada and Russia.

Details about Red's reanimated father

The last part of Noonan's section has Noonan at Red's house, where he is sitting at a table with Red and Red's zombie father (116–119). Red has Noonan pour a short drink for the old man (116). Red laughs about Noonan's choice in employees, and then:

> He fell silent and looked at the old man. A shudder crossed his face, and Noonan was amazed to see the look of real, sincere love and tenderness on that tough freckled mug of his....
>
> Guta came in, ordered Redrick to set the table, and set a large silver bowl with Noonan's favorite salad on the table.
>
> "Well, friends," Redrick announced. "Now we're going to have ourselves a feast!" (Bouis translation, 117–19)

Red seems to have a strong sentimental attachment to a now-dormant zombie. Noonan takes it all as a sick game being played.

The new translation fleshes out the scene considerably: as before, Red has Noonan pour a short drink for the old man, and Red and Noonan talk, but right after Red expresses his surprise that Noonan has put a lecher in charge of his prostitutes, the zombie stirs:

Here the old man, moving slowly and woodenly, like a giant doll, lifted his hand from his knee and dropped it on the table by his glass with a wooden bang. The hand was dark, with a bluish tint, and the clenching fingers made it look like a chicken foot. Redrick fell silent and looked at him. Something trembled in his face, and Noonan was amazed to see the most genuine, the most sincere love and affection expressed on that savage freckled mug....

Guta came in, ordered Redrick to set the table, and put down a large silver bowl with Noonan's favorite salad. And then the old man, in a single motion, as if someone had just remembered to pull the puppet strings, jerked the glass toward his open mouth.

"So, guys," said Redrick in a delighted voice, "now we'll have one hell of a party!" (Bormashenko translation, 152–55)

One can actually see the excision of the old translation here. As disturbing and eerie as it was with Red having sympathy for an inert zombie, the new translation with its vivid action is shocking.

Details about Dina and Red

In the final section of the novel, Red and Arthur are deep in the Zone. Red is mulling over the irony of having previously rescued Burbridge from the Zone, only to later find himself leading Burbridge's son Arthur into the most dangerous part of the Zone:

He was repelled by the thought and maybe that's why he started thinking about Arthur's sister. He just could not fathom it: how such a fantastic-looking woman could actually be a plastic fake, a dummy. It was like the buttons on his mother's blouse — they were amber, he remembered,

11

semitransparent and golden. He just wanted to shove them in his mouth and suck on them, and every time he was disappointed terribly, and every time he forgot about the disappointment. (Bouis translation, 121)

Red's complicated feelings about Burbridges senior and junior shifts to Dina, a young woman known throughout the town for throwing three-day parties, and then to illusory buttons on his mother's garment. It seems to move from concrete feelings about the men, through suppositions about the woman, to arrive at an abstraction regarding the disappointment between deceptive surfaces and reality, and the inability to learn from such disappointment.

The new translation is much more concrete:

Thinking about it was repellent, and maybe that was why he started thinking about Arthur's sister, about how he'd slept with this Dina — slept with her sober and slept with her drunk, and how every single time it'd been a disappointment. It was beyond belief; such a luscious broad, you'd think she was made for loving, but in actual fact she was nothing but an empty shell, a fraud, an inanimate doll instead of a woman. It reminded him of the buttons on his mother's jacket. (Bormashenko translation, 158)

The revelation that Red has had sex with Dina not once but many times is a devastating view of Red, as it destroys the implicit image that he is faithful to his wife, Guta. One of the few good traits that Red has is his devotion to his family: his wife, his mutant daughter, "Monkey," and even his zombie father.

Details about Monkey screaming

Marching deeper into the Zone, Red recalls the recent disturbance at home that led to his heavy drinking and finally the acceptance of this mission into the Zone:

> Only it hadn't been a dream. It was Monkey screaming in her bed by the window. Guta woke up, too, and took Redrick's hand. He could feel the sweat break out on her shoulder against his. They lay there and listened. (Bouis translation, 124)

Monkey's condition deteriorates in the course of the novel, with this screaming episode being the worst case. Rather than getting used to it, Red has been driven to drink and then to a terrible mission.

The new translation greatly expands the scene with just a few additional lines:

> Except that it wasn't a dream. It was the Monkey screaming, sitting on her bed by the window, and his father was responding from the other side of the house — very similarly, with creaky drawn-out cries, but with some kind of added gurgle. And they kept calling back and forth in the dark — it seemed to last a century, a hundred years, and another hundred years. Guta also woke up and held Redrick's hand, he felt her instantly clammy shoulder against his body, and they lay there for these hundreds and hundreds of years and listened. (Bormashenko translation, 163)

The zombie crying out adds eldritch horror to it.

Roughing it in the Zone

The expedition of Red and Arthur in the last section is somewhat like a camping trip. As the night fades, it is time to start the day:

> Redrick got up, went behind the ore car, sat on the embankment, and watched as the green wash dimmed and quickly turned to pink. (Bouis translation, 127)

Red here watches the weird Zone-phenomenon of the pre-dawn "green wash."

The new translation gives a less philosophical version of events:

> Redrick got up and, unbuckling his belt, said, "Aren't you going to relieve yourself? Keep in mind, we might not have another chance."
>
> He walked behind the railcar, squatted on the embankment, and, grunting, watched as the green glow quickly faded. (Bormashenko translation, 167)

•

The new edition includes an afterword by Boris Strugatsky, the surviving brother/author. His notes on the Soviet censorship make it clear why the passages I found had been cut. Editors told the brothers to "take the reanimated corpses out" (203), which would lead to the severe reduction of action for Red's zombie father; the editors compiled "Comments Concerning the Immoral Behavior of the Heroes" (203-4) and "Comments About Vulgarisms and Slang Expressions" (204), which would cover Red's adultery with Dina, and roughing it in the Zone, respectively.

Names for Artifacts and Characters

While I am very enthusiastic about the new passages, there are other changes that I am not so happy with. No doubt this is partially due to my having read the old translation many times, but I am unhappy with the new terms for the artifacts: Spitting devil's cabbage becomes Satan's blossom;

Flying boot (a vehicle) becomes Hoverboot; Witches' jelly becomes Hell slime; the Golden Ball becomes the Golden Sphere; Black sprays become Black sparks; the eternal battery "So-so" (90) becomes Spacell (116); Jolly ghosts (107) become Happy ghosts (138); Zombies (108) become Living corpses (138).

The old way was much more rooted in fairy tale sensibilities, as is plain with "flying boot," "witches' jelly," and most importantly, "Golden Ball." "Spitting devil's cabbage" gives me an immediate image, whereas "Satan's blossom" is rather vague. In contemporary usage, "slime" is simply used too often, in the moral sense as well as the mock-literal sense tracing back to *Ghostbusters*.

There are also new names for some of the characters. For instance, Buzzard Burbridge is now Vulture Burbridge, while Hamster is now Gopher. I prefer the alliteration of "Buzzard Burbridge," as well as the proximity of "buzzard" to "bastard." On the other hand, "Gopher" is better than "Hamster," which sounds too cute for what is really a mangled ex-stalker who acts as Burbridge's crippled butler. Extra bonus for the fact that "gopher" is a homonym for "gofer," one who goes for things on command. (Then again, because "Hamster" is cute it might still win out as the nickname for a pathetic cripple, as I hope to explain next.)

I am not writing about the original text in Russian, which I have not read; I am only talking about my impression of the text through the old translation. My sense of it was that the stalkers are initially presented as being just like prospectors braving a dangerous environment in order to obtain riches — as such, stalker culture seemed to me to be like prospector culture, being colorful, direct, and superstitious. The fact that stalker terminology seemed to come from fairy tales gave many nuances to this — first, that fairy tales are deeply steeped in superstition; and second, the alien stuff was so alien as to require such a lexicon granted by the "familiar/weird" language of fairy tales. (For their part, the scientists in the text use the more science fictional tactic of naming things in technological terms.)

The "stalker names" they use are typical nicknames: "Red" is called this because he has red hair; "Four Eyes" wears glasses; and so on. But the finer point is that the group assigns such names, they are not self-selected. We know for a fact that Burbridge did not give himself the name of a scavenger bird — it used to be something else, but so many of his stalker partners had died with him in the Zone that the group re-named him after the ominous bird and warned him that he better not come back alone again (old 130; new 172), which is why he then saved the stalker who became his crippled butler. Thus, my sense of the name is that it is mocking, yet also a warning to Burbridge and others who deal with him.

As the novel progresses, the stalkers are revealed to be (or they actually become in time) more like gangsters. This adds to the sense of naming conventions: look to the gangsters of *The Sopranos* and see such deprecating names as "Big Pussy."

So in the prospector/gangster mode, wherein a big fellow might reasonably be given the nickname "Tiny," it might make more sense for the mangled colleague to be called "cutie pie" (hamster) rather than "ugly rodent" (gopher).

I only say this much to explain my reading.

I have no wish to argue with the translator Olena Bormashenko. She read the text in Russian and wanted to do a better job of presenting it in English. She asked Boris and he gave her the uncut version to work with, and then when Chicago Review Press asked Boris for reprint rights, he sent them to her. Now the book is out and that's a fine thing.

For those who have never read it before, this is the best time to read it. For those who read it before, this is a great opportunity to read it again, for the first time as the authors truly intended it.

THE POLITICS OF *ROADSIDE PICNIC*

The Russian novel *Roadside Picnic* was first published in 1972 and translated into English in 1977. Its Swedish edition won a Jules Verne award and in 1981 it received an award for best foreign novel of the year at the Festival du Science Fiction in Metz. Over multiple re-readings of the 1977 translation in 2011, my sense of the politics of *Roadside Picnic* altered considerably. A breakthrough came this year when a new translation was published and I read the new edition's foreword by Ursula K. Le Guin and the afterword by Boris Strugatsky.

Le Guin revisits the context of the novel, telling what a refreshing text it was in the 1970s, written as if the authors Arkady and Boris Strugatsky were "indifferent to ideology" (vi). In contrast, Boris Strugatsky's piece is about the complicated publication history of *Roadside Picnic* as a book in the USSR and the long-running arguments with the Soviet censors. If I understand it correctly, the censors were not concerned with the ideology, since the novel's ideology was purely Soviet orthodox. As Strugastsky repeatedly told them,

the novel contained nothing criminal; it was quite

ideologically appropriate and certainly not dangerous in that sense. And the fact that the world depicted in it was coarse, cruel, and hopeless, well, that was how it had to be — it was the world of "decaying capitalism and triumphant bourgeois ideology." (207)

It was precisely the graphic coarseness, vulgarity, and immoral behavior in the novel that was the problem for the censors. This material may have been acceptable for a literary journal like *Avrora* (where *Roadside Picnic* was serialized in 1972), but publication as a young adult title was a different matter.

Roadside Picnic is about humans dealing with weird artifacts left on Earth after a mysterious alien visit. The aliens are never seen nor are their vehicles; there are just the six Zones scattered across the globe where they visited, and the strange objects left behind. (The novel's title comes from one theory about the Visit — that it was merely a roadside picnic, and the artifacts are only alien trash.) The Zones are dangerous, filled with weird monsters and deadly traps, but adventurers called "stalkers" sneak in to bring out artifacts they can sell. The novel is a series of episodes over a span of years following a stalker named Red.

Initially I took *Roadside Picnic* to be an action story that was, for a Soviet work, remarkably free of politics. It was a page-turning thriller, with a heady mixture of elements from film noir, the fey logic of Wonderland, and even scenes from the Bible. The novel does an incredible job of shifting around: At the beginning, stalkers seem to be like prospectors who undertake personal risk in order to win their gold; then they more closely resemble gangsters trafficking in contraband; finally they are revealed to be still worse. Humor is used as a setup for a dark surprise, time and time again in the tale. The opening interview suggests that mass hysteria and wild rumors exaggerated the alien arrival, but as Red enters the Zone in the next section, he offhandedly reveals that the reality of the Visit was far worse than what was ridiculed in the radio show. Nearly every section also has a dark surprise about its hero, too, whether it be that good-guy Red has just smuggled a weapon of mass destruction out of the Zone or that bumbling bureaucrat Dick Noonan is also a brutal whoremaster working for the secret police.

By the third reading, though, I began to perceive Soviet details. For example, a wall is put up to protect the humans from the Zone, and it seems inconceivable that this was not related to the Berlin Wall. I resisted this, because such a reading reduces the Zone to mere "capitalism," the stalkers to being simple smugglers, and the wondrous alien artifacts to being only lipstick, blue jeans, and rock music — items of everyday Western "decadence" that worked their way into the USSR and "polluted" it. This transmutes the wonder into a typical anti-bourgeoisie rant. And yet, I was forced to conclude that ultimately the work is a devastating jeremiad by a pair of communist utopians earnestly warning about the horrors of capitalism.

This interpretation seemed to be a "magic key," possibly capable of unlocking the text's intractable mysteries, so I researched whether it was already in common use or not.

Fredric Jameson's *Archaeologies of the Future* (2005) says of *Roadside Picnic:*

> This text moves in a space beyond the facile and obligatory references to the two rival social systems [capitalism and communism]; and it cannot be coherently decoded as yet another *samizdat* message or expression of liberal political protest by Soviet dissidents. (294)

Jameson states it is not a simple and obvious case, which seems rather cagey to me, but he points out that the text is not anti-Soviet. On this last item, Landon's *Science Fiction After 1900* (1995) agrees: "nor were the Strugatskys ever dissidents or anti-Soviet" (96).

Roland Boer, in *Knockin' on Heaven's Door* (1999), goes further: after describing how the brothers had been blacklisted for the unauthorized 1972 publication of their novel *The Ugly Swans* in West Germany, he writes, "Yet, it would be a mistake to see the Strugatskys as dissidents in the Soviet era, a view that led in part to the flood of translations and publications of their works in the 1970s" (111). In this way Boer claims that a misperception of the brothers as dissidents is what led to their being embraced by the West in the first place.

The notion of the Strugatskys operating within a Western ideological blind spot is picked up by Stephen W. Potts in *The Second Marxian Invasion* (1991), where, on the topic of the Strugatsky novel *Space Apprentice,* he writes: "Despite Theodore Sturgeon's contention (in his introduction to the 1981 Macmillan edition) that this novel contains very little Marxism, it is in fact wholly dialectical" (20). Potts continues this topic of ardent Marxism with regard to *Roadside Picnic:* "gangsterism is closely tied to capitalism in Marxist thought; since both are geared to the accumulation of material wealth to the exclusion of other values, one is merely a form of the other. This connection is evident in the behavior of Red and his colleagues and contacts" (78); and, "Of all the works of the Strugatsky brothers, *Roadside Picnic* provides the strongest criticism of the capitalist ethic" (80).

Finally, the highly influential Istvan Csicsery-Ronay, Jr. wrote in 1986 that *Roadside Picnic* is "a fable of the despair of the '60s [Russian] intelligentsia facing the complete destruction of the [Soviet] reform movement" and sees it as "the convergence of Eastern and Western ennui, the fruit of global acquiescence to purely material satisfactions and the abdication of all higher moral purposes — the victory of 'realism' over utopian idealism" ("Towards the

Last Fairy Tale," *Science Fiction Studies #38).* This is encoded, but I read it as asserting that *Roadside Picnic* is a firmly pro-communist utopian work that rails against the anti-utopian West.

A summary of this survey is like examining the layers of an onion: we see that the Strugatskys were taken to be Soviet dissidents by the West's *hoi polloi;* then Jameson, Landon, and Boer aver the brothers are not anti-Soviet, which implies a type of political neutrality; while Csicsery-Ronay and Potts claim the brothers are really quite pro-Soviet, demolishing the pretense of neutrality.

I find myself in the camp of Csicsery-Ronay and Potts. To develop my reading further, I will start with the wall at the Zone. In Section 1, bureaucrat Dick Noonan tells stalker Red,

> They're starting a lot of construction. The Institute's putting up three new buildings, and they're also going to wall off the Zone from the cemetery to the old ranch. The good times for stalkers are coming to an end. (46)

Section 1 is set thirteen years after the Visit, that moment when the six Zones appeared on Earth. When Section 2 begins, eighteen years after the Visit, we find Red and Vulture at the cemetery, two stalkers hiding in the shadow of the nine-foot tall wall. So the Institute was talking about building a wall in Year 13, and in Year 18 the wall is in place, apparently with a stalker hole through it already.

Roadside Picnic takes place in the fictional Canadian mining town of Harmont. The Harmont Zone, "a belt of empty land fifty miles across" (110), has overlapped perhaps half of the town at one edge. The text is very quiet about which half of Harmont is located in the Zone, but based on movements to and from, it seems to be the west side. I interpret the clues such that the Institute, the legal gateway into the Zone, is situated at the midpoint of the wall that stretches north to the abandoned ranch and south to the cemetery.

The timeline of the Zone wall's construction has an eerie echo in that of the Berlin Wall, which was built in 1961, sixteen years after the end of World War Two. The Berlin Wall completely encircled West Berlin, and while the Zone's wall does not surround the entire Zone, still west Harmont seems to be in the Zone. These points suggest that the story's hidden internal date is 1958 to 1966, and that Harmont is a stand-in for divided Berlin.

Moving from the Berlin Wall itself, the items that were routinely smuggled into East Germany from the West is a bewildering laundry list of commonplace items: newspapers, magazines, recorded materials, films, radios, medicine, cosmetics, and Western clothing. The newspapers and magazines especially jump out as likely artifacts from a real "roadside picnic," but otherwise it is difficult to match up any of these products with the wondrous alien artifacts from the Zone: the empties, the full empties, the spacells (self-multiplying batteries), the bracelets (which confer health benefits), the hoops (which exhibit perpetual motion), the black sparks (worn by citizens as jewelry), the sponges, the shriekers, the pins (which "talk" when squeezed), the jars of carbonated clay, the rattling napkins, and the lobster eyes.

"Pins that talk" easily fit into the category of "recorded materials," i.e., vinyl records that talk via needles. "Lobster eyes" could be contact lenses. The "black sparks" (called "black sprays" in the 1977 translation), used as feminine ornamentation, are probably an encrypted version of false eyelashes or mascara.

The spacells, which reproduce in a quasi-biological manner, remind me of a detail from Fritz Leiber's short story "Myths My Great-Granddaughter Taught Me" (1963), in which the narrator is being quizzed on Norse mythology by a strange girl who reinterprets each magical device with a scientific explanation:

> "And the gold ring Draupnir, that dropped eight rings like itself every ninth night — "
>
> "That could be atomic transmutation," she said thoughtfully, "or maybe just the capitalist economic system as it dreams of itself." (310)

That is, the self-reproducing spacells strike me as a Soviet view of the capitalist system "as it dreams of itself," creating wealth out of nothing, contrary to the zero-sum game expounded by communism. The same holds for the perpetual-motion hoops.

This tracing of low-level artifacts to black market consumer goods in the USSR may be haphazard, but I have a much greater degree of confidence in tracking the high-level artifact called "hell slime." For Section 2, the military-industrialists commission the two stalkers Red and Vulture to fetch some of this notoriously dangerous stuff. In doing the job, Vulture's legs are splashed with hell slime and they rapidly waste away into a rubbery material. Red still sells the slime to his patrons. They, in turn, put it into a specially designed facility called Carrigan Labs, which subsequently suffers a disaster when the slime gets out of control: "thirty-five dead, more than a hundred injured, and the entire laboratory is completely unusable" (135).

Hell slime seems to be the equivalent of a weapon of mass destruction, so it is probably a code for the atomic bomb, first developed in the West. The Soviet atomic bomb project used spies in the West from 1942 to 1945, and the first Soviet bomb was tested in 1949. So Red and Vulture are analogous to atomic spies. The novel's Carrigan Labs accident seems like the USSR's Kyshtym Disaster of 1957, a military-industrial mishap that is currently the third-worst nuclear accident after Chernobyl (1986) and Fukushima (2011).

So, by this reading, the Zone is capitalism, the wall is

the Berlin Wall, and hell slime is the atom bomb. Next I will touch on how *Roadside Picnic* is a different kind of alien-invasion novel.

•

The seminal alien-invasion novel, Wells' 1898 *The War of the Worlds,* gives us the storm of (heat-ray) guns, (Martian) steel, and (plucky Earth) germs. In sharp contrast, *Roadside Picnic* presents a soft invasion, something like the coca-colonization implied by the list of Western goods in the Soviet black market. At the same time there are strong hints of a slow-motion invasion along the lines of botanical propagation, vermin eradication, and plague.

In the botanical analogy, the artifacts can be seen as alien seeds, with the stalkers then recast as birds and squirrels, transporting the seeds and accidentally planting some of them. The first artifact encountered in the text is the empty, a cylindrical force field with a copper disk at each end. When the stalkers find a full empty, there is a fluid inside, described as "blue filling swirling slowly" (31) and "blue syrup" (32). Red says the context makes it plain that an empty is a container, but one might also call it a husk or eggshell. When Red later finds the Golden Sphere, he notes that, despite its name, its color is "closer to copper" (188). Thus it seems possible that the empties are seeds/eggs of the Golden Sphere.

In the vermin eradication analogy, the artifacts are like those sweet poison ant traps where the worker ants carry the tasty poison back to the queen, thereby dooming the entire colony. The Zones might be the beachheads for an impersonal alien terraforming project.

Then there is the plague model. Plague terms are used to describe the effects of the Visit (for example, the Plague Quarter is the first neighborhood of the Zone from the Institute), but such a model can be extended far beyond the day of the Visit. The text tells of an emigrant effect (139–40) wherein people from Harmont who move away are followed by uncanny coincidences that harm those around them. This weirdness is never resolved, yet it seems as though each emigrant is a Typhoid Mary who, having successfully survived the Zone plague, is now a carrier of the same strangeness in a smaller scale.

In *The War of the Worlds,* a shooting star in the sky, an impact crater on the ground, and a spaceship in that crater mark the arrival of the Martians. *Roadside Picnic* has none of this — no signs in the sky, no crater, no vehicle or remnant of one. This fits perfectly with Dr. Pillman's theory in the text of a "roadside picnic": the vehicle and the aliens are gone; all that is left behind is their incidental trash.

We have few clues about what the Visit was like. For the vast majority of people it seems to have been taken as a hoax, as Dr. Pillman reports about his own initial reaction (2). For those caught in the suddenly created Zone, there was something real and immediate, yet the evidence suggests that effects were highly localized: in the Plague Quarter the people caught a "disease" that later made their skin peel off and their fingernails fall out (21); in the three Blind Quarters adjacent to the Plague Quarter there were said to be some bright flashes, yet the people caught permanent night-blindness from a loud thunder (22).

•

Having argued that *Roadside Picnic* is a profoundly pro-Soviet work and that it describes a slow yet deadly invasion, I would like to cap it all off by showing how *Roadside Picnic* is surprisingly like a Soviet version of Blish's *Black Easter* — a science fictional treatment on the literal arrival of Satan on Earth.

The satanic elements of *Roadside Picnic* show up early in the text, in full view and not encoded. The first mention is in "Satan's blossom," a spitting plant of the Zone (18). Then there is the character Gutalin, the quixotic counter-stalker who buys up artifacts and returns them to the Zone. Gutalin preaches that Satan put the Zone there to tempt humans, and that the artifacts are Satan's toys. As he says in Section 1:

And futile are the prayers of the worshippers of Satan. And only those who renounce him shall be saved. Thou, of human flesh, whom Satan has seduced, who play with his toys and covet his treasures — I tell thee, thou art blind! ... Stamp on the devil's baubles. (44)

Gutalin declares that doom is near, "Because the pale horse has been saddled, and the rider has put a foot in the stirrup" (44). This is an allusion to the Fourth Horseman of the Apocalypse, a figure in the Bible's book of Revelation (6:8). It turns out to be a foreshadowing of many details shared between Revelation and *Roadside Picnic*.

• The resurrection of the dead is a part of Revelation, which finds a mockery in the reanimated corpses of *Roadside Picnic* (including Red's zombie father).

• Revelation tells of demonic "miracles," including non-divine healings (13:12), which translates into Vulture's answered wishes and his hope for new legs from the Golden Sphere.

• Revelation says that the Beast "maketh fire come down from heaven on the earth in sight of man" (13:13), and *Roadside Picnic* has Red and Arthur attacked by demonic lightning that goes sideways between two hills (179–80).

• Revelation describes a false prophet and an idol made in the image of the Beast of the Sea, an idol that comes to life and kills those who do not worship it (13:14, 15). This is close to Vulture as false prophet and the Golden Sphere as idol, especially in how the artifact seems to come to life for Red with aquatic detail: "to dance in place like a buoy in the waves" (192).

The links between Revelation and *Roadside Picnic* show that in order to transmit the apocalypse of their vision the brothers Strugatsky lifted bits from the Bible's apocalypse. But they took more from the Bible than just that.

The action in the final section, with Red and Arthur trudging deep into the Zone, reminds me of Abraham taking his son Isaac up the mountain to sacrifice him to God (Genesis 22). Yet the analogy is not quite right, since Arthur is not Red's son. Sacrificing "someone else's son" sounds like a warped version of the crucifixion of Jesus, and there are some strange Jesus-like details to Arthur.

Red's daughter Monkey, along with Vulture's offspring, Dina and Arthur, are all children directly affected by the Zone. Monkey has been cursed with a mutation that causes her to devolve over time into an animal. Through Vulture's wishes and human sacrifices, the Golden Sphere has blessed both of Vulture's children: Dina has been given physical beauty as well as an attitude that makes her a good stand-in for the Whore of Babylon (another figure from Revelation); whereas Arthur seems to be genuinely good, a paragon of innocence, idealism, and altruism. The three offspring of stalkers are thus partially children of the Zone. So Red's feeding of Arthur to the grinder guarding the Golden Sphere is a perversion of Jesus being offered up to his father, God, in exchange for universal redemption.

From this angle, with Red sacrificing Arthur in a satanic parody, it looks like a very black Easter indeed. Such a reading also provides a logical solution to the vexing problems regarding the arrival of the Zones, since if they came up from infernal regions like fairy rings rather than coming down from the sky like meteors, there would be no shooting stars, no craters, and no vehicles.

•

Now we come to the famous enigmatic ending, and the curious way in which this text has been perceived in the USA. The very first note is emblematic of all I've seen:

> The Strugatskys' deft and supple handling of loyalty and greed, of friendship and love, of despair and frustration and loneliness [produces] a truly superb tale, ending most poignantly in what can only be called a blessing—Theodore Sturgeon, introducing the 1977 edition

"Can *only* be called a blessing?" No. This is too far overboard for me to tolerate. "*Might* be called a blessing" is a form I'm more comfortable with, but even then it raises many questions.

It boils down to how one interprets the abrupt ending of the novel. If one believes that the Golden Sphere grants wishes, and that Red really is a sort of Galahad who just found the Grail, then the device bestows Utopia on Earth, and reality as we know it ends as suddenly as the text with the ascent of mankind to superman or angelhood.

If one doubts that the dingus grants wishes or believes that the wishes are as limited as Vulture suggests (such that Red's wish is clearly impossible), then what you have is more like a wild savage who has just committed human sacrifice to an evil idol that is demonstrably taking over the world on its own. Witness the descent of modern man to primitive, bloodcurdling superstition.

So by my reasoning, Sturgeon must see the utopian ending and feels that "the ends justify the means," that is, murder of Arthur is bad, but it is worth it for the worldwide good of the utopia.

I would be curious to find a published Soviet reading that finds the ending utopian or even "ambiguous," as I suspect the majority took it as unambiguously anti-capitalist. Room for further research.

****

Works Cited

Boer, Roland. *Knockin' on Heaven's Door*. London; New York: Routledge, 1991.

Csicsery-Ronay, Istvan, Jr. "Towards the Last Fairy Tale." *Science Fiction Studies #38*. Greencastle, Indiana: DePauw University, March 1986.

Jameson, Fredric. *Archaeologies of the Future*. London: Verso, 2007.

Landon, Brooks. *Science Fiction After 1900*. New York: Routledge, 2002.

Leiber, Fritz. "Myths My Great-Granddaughter Taught Me" (1963). In *Worlds of Fritz Leiber*. Boston: Gregg Press, 1979.

Potts, Stephen W. *The Second Marxian Invasion*. San Bernardino, California: Borgo Press, 1991.

Strugatsky, Arkady and Boris. *Roadside Picnic*. Translated by Olena Bormashenko. Chicago: Chicago Review Press, 2012.

———. *Roadside Picnic*. Translated by Antonina W. Bouis (1977). Gollancz S.F. Masterworks Edition. London: Orion, 2007.

Wells, H.G. *The War of the Worlds*. 1898.

STALKY V. STALKER, OR, *STALKY &*
CO. AGAINST *ROADSIDE PICNIC*

In "The Strugatskys' Traditional Science Fiction Revisited, Part 1" Patrick L. McGuire makes note of a Kipling connection to the early development of the brothers Arkady and Boris Strugatsky: "It turns out that Arkady in 1952 had been intrigued by the Kipling novella 'Stalky & Co.,' which is fairly obscure even in the Anglosphere and decidedly obscure in Russia" (*The New York Review of Science Fiction #302*, 20).

Boris Strugatsky addresses this during his 2012 Afterword to *Roadside Picnic*:

> In his tender years Arkady, who was still a student at the Military Institute for Foreign Languages, received from me a copy of Kipling's *Stalky & Co.* that I happened to pick up at a flea market; he read it, was delighted, and right then made a rough translation ... which became one of my favorite books of my school and college years. (197)

So it was a gift from Boris to his older brother, and Arkady was so enthused over it that he translated the book as a gift for Boris, who came to love it himself. Years later the Brothers Strugatsky wrote *Roadside Picnic*, which at the very least appropriated the English term "stalker" from the name of Kipling's crafty character Stalky.

Boris notes the Kipling work as a novel; McGuire names it a novella; still others call it a collection. Technically it might be termed a fix-up, since it is a collection of eight stories that were published first in magazines, then artfully assembled into a book of nine episodes (one story having been divided in two).

Whatever you call it, count me as among those who had never even heard of *Stalky & Co.* until mentioned this way in regards to the brothers. After several such mentions I was curious enough to downloaded a copy, and soon I found myself laughing out loud.

I can see why the Strugatskys liked it so much, as I find *Stalky* to be powerful stuff. Set among boys at a Victorian boarding school, the "company" is really a group of three teens, each with strengths and weaknesses, led by the wily Stalky. Pooling their talents, they do each other's schoolwork. They break rules by using tobacco, building forts in the bushes, and sniping animals with saloon pistols, yet they avoid detection from the school authorities. They detest cricket along with other forms of fake patriotism, and while they maintain a low profile, they still exact poetic revenge for slights they suffer. All of this amounts to hilarious adventure. And even though their handiwork is so crafty as to leave no traces leading back to them, the school Head nearly always canes them for it, a punishment they accept as part of the game, bearing no hard feelings for the Head.

So I see *Stalky* as a delightful mixture of Twain's *Tom Sawyer* and *Huckleberry Finn*, along with *The Three Musketeers*, all placed within an institutional setting that alternates between merely degrading and decidedly prison-like. The autobiographical fiction is subversive on many levels: the boys work against authority, and they mercilessly criticize the popular boarding-school fictions of the day for painting too rosy a picture. Also subversive is the fact that the corporal punishment is not a deterrent as either a threat or a punishment: it is merely the price to be paid if they are willing to play their pranks.

The trio are heroes of the stories, but we see dark sides to them, too, and we also have intimations of how much they suffered in their first years at the school before they formed their team. But as the stories progress, we learn that their particular school is a portal to military service. The boys are keen to hear of former classmates serving overseas in Afghanistan and India, and they honor dead men who were just a few years their senior. This sense of honor, duty, and service to others adds a somber nobility to the boys, balancing their anarchic antics.

I found reading *Stalky* to be an adventure in that the Victorian institutions and school slang have been rendered so strange and exotic by the passage of a century. I suppose that it was similarly foreign to the Brothers Strugatsky, crossing the lines of culture, but also note that Arkady was in a military institute, which must have been close to what goes on in the novel. McGuire reports that after Arkady graduated from high school, he was drafted, and then transferred to the Military Foreign Language Institute in 1943 at the age of eighteen. The Institute in question:

> had a high washout rate because of the difficulty of the subject matter. Arkady coped fairly well with the academic side, thanks to a normal amount of effort plus what proved to be a huge talent for foreign languages. However … he frequently found himself in minor trouble for disciplinary infractions, these partly … deriving from girl-chasing and partly … from sloppy military dress and demeanor. (*The New York Review of Science Fiction #302*, 12)

It would seem that Arkady's life at the Institute was a fairly close match to that of Stalky's rebels at their school.

In any event, around twenty years after Boris sent Arkady the book, they wrote their own take on *Stalky* in the form of *Roadside Picnic*. Some elements remain the same, while other elements are shifted.

One aspect that carries through is the overall structure. *Stalky* is episodic, taking place over the trio's last few years at the school, with an epilogue showing a view of their lives in the field. *Roadside Picnic* has five sections across many years, ending with a view of the hero's life in the field. Still, the Brothers accentuate their sections by having different point of view characters for each, and different tenses, whereas *Stalky* is uniform.

On the other hand, the Brothers Strugatsky make a clear shift by changing the schoolboys into prospector/gangsters. Among stalkers there is no honor, there is no duty, there is no service to others: there is treachery, backstabbing, skullduggery. There is no trio of friends, no new Musketeers; instead the motto is "every man for himself" in a dog-eat-dog world. Even so, the Brothers manage to maintain enough moral ambiguity that the reader is still shocked when the hero does some villainous act.

Another big difference is that the Brothers Strugatsky trade the humor for horror. *Stalky* has distant Afghanistan, which *Roadside Picnic* translates into the very-close Zone.

So in the end, where Kipling has his boys go through moral ambiguity to emerge as truly good men (or men who turn their pranks into good service for the British Empire), the Brothers Strugatsky have their hero fail a series of moral tests to arrive at a moral ambiguity of hell, or possibly heaven.

****

Works Cited

Kipling, Rudyard. *Stalky & Co.* 1899.

McGuire, Patrick L. "The Strugatskys' Traditional Science Fiction Revisited, Part 1." *The New York Review of Science Fiction #302*. New York: Burrowing Wombat Press, October 2013.

Strugatsky, Arkady and Boris. *Roadside Picnic*. Translated by Olena Bormashenko. Chicago: Chicago Review Press, 2012.

THE LOST STRUGATSKY TRIPTYCH:
UNINTENDED MEETINGS

In 1971 the Brothers Strugatsky proposed a single-volume, curious collection:

> This putative anthology was called *Unintended Meetings*, was dedicated to the problem of humanity's contact with another intelligence, and consisted of three novels, two finished — *Dead Mountaineer's Hotel* and *Space Mowgli* — and one [*Roadside Picnic*] that was still being written. (Afterword to Bormashenko's translation of *Roadside Picnic*, 198)

After an exhausting epic of struggle,

> The *Unintended Meetings* anthology saw the light of day in the autumn of 1980, disfigured, massacred, and pathetic. The only thing remaining from the original plan was *Space Mowgli; Dead Mountaineer's Hotel* had been lost on the field of battle more than five years before, while the *Picnic* had undergone such editing that the authors wanted neither to read

it nor even simply to flip through its pages. (209)

So the dream died, and for decades the fate of the three elements remained uncertain in English translation. The planetary adventure novella *Space Mowgli* was published in English in 1982 (as part of the omnibus *Escape Attempt)*, with a translation that has no controversy about it. The alien-artifact-scavenging, pocket epic *Roadside Picnic* received a definitive translation in 2012. The detective parody/homage *Dead Mountaineer's Hotel* had a fresh translation in 2015 as *Dead Mountaineer's Inn: One More Last Rite for the Detective Genre.*

Now that I have read and enjoyed the three novels, I can say how crazy is the idea of the *Unintended Meetings* anthology. It is *moon bat* crazy. Through most of the filters I try, I end up seeing two novels that fit and one that does not. Try "mash-up works" to pair *Mountaineer* and *Roadside Picnic,* but not *Mowgli,* which is standard genre. Try "sf" (or "Kipling") and pair *Roadside Picnic* and *Mowgli,* but not *Mountaineer.* Come up with something to pair *Mowgli* and *Mountaineer,* but not *Roadside Picnic:* "standard tropes," perhaps?

The one filter that definitely works is the one that Boris stated: "the problem of humanity's contact with another intelligence." Which means it is thematic in a cross-genre way. Which to me reinforces the suspicion that it is more properly a triptych.

But even so, it is crazy. I cannot figure out how they thought this would fly. The genre differences are just too great: a reader who wanted the *Forbidden Planet* adventure of *Mowgli* would probably hate the other two novels, and so on.

One toehold I have is Stanislaw Lem's notion that sf is Literature (or should be). Maybe the Brothers were going with this. But again, it is crazy: the *Unintended Meetings* of their dreams seems too "genre" for the literature crowd; too "anti-genre" (and/or "multi-genre") for the genre crowd.

The reason Lem comes to mind is that, as I was reading *Dead Mountaineer's Inn,* a few chapters in I started seeing similarities to Lem's famous *Solaris* (1961). The inn seems as if it is haunted by the ghost of the mountaineer whose tragic fall gave the place its name, the way the station in *Solaris* seems like it is haunted by unquiet spirits. The people at the inn are so quirky that they seem increasingly like friends of the Mad Hatter; the scientists at the station are going mad from the ghosts.

I wondered if the Brothers were playing a double game where on the surface they were mocking detective fiction, but beneath this they were knocking *Solaris* all over the place. The problem with this theory is that *Solaris* is already known to be a haunted house/mystery scenario, so on the Venn diagram it shares the same mash-up roots as *Mountaineer.*

Putting that aside, the "alien contact" thread leads straight through the maze: all three novels have it, each in a different way.

Dead Mountaineer's Inn proves to be a thriller that races along the parody/homage track like a comedy version of *Sleuth* (1972). What seems an impossible mystery for the mundane world is quickly solved when the criminals turn out to be aliens from another world. Helicopter snipers gun them down as they try to escape. The innkeeper dutifully changes the name of the place to "the Interstellar Zombie Inn" so as to reflect the new reality or crassly capitalize upon it.

Although the title of *Space Mowgli* sounds like an adventure based on the hero of Kipling's Jungle Book stories, as I intimated before, the story is really more like *Forbidden Planet* (1956). To wit: a starship comes to a lifeless planet, and the human team begins terraforming it. A few individuals begin having weird experiences, including hearing noises and voices and seeing ghostly images. This phase resolves when they realize the world has a crashed human ship, which had one survivor: a boy raised from infancy by the unseen aliens. This child is the Space Mowgli, and the humans hope he will be a bridge between human and alien.

But to use the kid as a key, the humans have to re-awaken the human side of the boy, which proves tricky and traumatic. The philosophical problem is that while the kid is a presumed pet to the aliens and a potential utensil for the humans, neither role is realistically best for him.

So instead of being an adventure story about an animal-friend hero like Tarzan, this is a view of the feral kid as an object, a victim. The humans express criticism against the alien foster parents for what they have done to him, psychologically as well as physically, since he has been surgically modified. A faction among the humans worries that trying to use the kid as a tool is further victimization.

But in the next twist, the humans discover that the planet had been marked "off limits" by a previous starfaring culture: thus they have inadvertently trespassed into a forbidden zone, and the story doubles down on the *Forbidden Planet* aspect. So *Mowgli* ends with a hasty retreat of the humans, a mirror image of the alien escape attempt at the end of *Mountaineer*.

Where *Mountaineer* and *Mowgli* amount to "close encounters" of the brief kind, *Roadside Picnic* is decidedly long haul, showing the changes wrought on human society and specific individuals over many years.

Roadside Picnic is famous for being about "unintended meetings" since it is all about humans on Earth picking over the enigmatic alien artifacts that, in perhaps a best-case scenario, are the trash left behind by interstellar travelers who only stopped for a brief picnic.

So there you have it. The novels share a theme. They also share a sense of weird, expressed as ghosts in *Mountaineer* and *Mowgli*, and more fairy-fey in *Roadside Picnic*. Even so, the dream of the Brothers Strugatsky to combine the three works into *Unintended Meetings* seems enigmatic and strange, seemingly an artifact of a liminal realm at the borders of genres and literature: as amusing as *Dead Mountaineer's Inn;* as brooding as *Space Mowgli;* as darkling as *Roadside Picnic.*

****

Works cited

Strugatsky, Arkady and Boris. *Dead Mountaineer's Inn: One More Last Rite for the Detective Genre.* Translated by Josh Billings. Brooklyn: Melville House Publishing, 2015.

———. *Escape Attempt* ("Escape Attempt," "The Kid from Hell," and "Space Mowgli"). Translated by Roger DeGaris. New York: Macmillan Publishing, 1982.

———. *Roadside Picnic.* Translated by Olena Bormashenko. Chicago: Chicago Review Press, 2012.

SEARCHING FOR THE WORST
EDITION OF *ROADSIDE PICNIC*

Roadside Picnic had a difficult journey in Russian publication: after being a magazine serial in 1972, eight years of struggle later it finally appeared in book form as part of the *Unintended Meetings* ("Nenaznachennye Vstrechi") anthology of 1980. Boris Strugatsky wrote movingly about how bad that version was:

> The *Unintended Meetings* anthology saw the light of day in the autumn of 1980, disfigured, massacred, and pathetic. The only thing remaining from the original plan [of an omnibus containing *Roadside Picnic, Dead Mountaineer's Hotel,* and *Space Mowgli*] was *Space Mowgli* ... while the *Picnic* had undergone such editing that the authors wanted neither to read it nor even simply to flip through its pages.... to this day, I find the *Unintended Meetings* anthology unpleasant to even hold in my hands, never mind read. (Bormashenko translation of *Roadside Picnic*, 208–9)

Such sentiments from the co-author made me believe

that the *Unintended Meetings* version was the worst edition of all, in terms of excised material, and I was curious to see how it would compare with the English editions.

In a Russian Wikipedia article on *Roadside Picnic* (https://ru.wikipedia.org/wiki/) I found hints that the problems with the *Unintended Meetings* edition were less about censorship and more about sloppy editing: the town's name "Harmont" was inexplicably changed to "Marmont," and the name of a stalker gang was altered from Warr to Fan (or "BaPP" to "BeeP"). (This gang is one of many mentioned by Mr. Lemchen in the Noonan section of the novel. It is not "Quasimodo," it is a group immediately before Quasimodo, rendered "Varr" in the Bormashenko translation.)

I obtained a copy of *Unintended Meetings*. It has three works: "The Visitors" (1958), *Roadside Picnic,* and *Space Mowgli* (1971). I read "The Visitors" in English translation in *Aliens, Travelers, and Other Strangers* (1984), and it does not relate to the aliens of *Roadside Picnic,* it is about a flying saucer encountered in the middle of the desert.

Turning to the notorious edition of *Roadside Picnic,* I confirm the existence of the "Marmont" and "BeeP" typos. My plan was to spot-check four areas of the text that had shown obvious variation between the Bouis translation (1977) and the Bormashenko translation (2012). These four areas are:

1. The mention of a Russian Zone. (This passage comes when Noonan is in transit to his café and is musing on Singapore.)
2. The zombie father taking a drink. (This line comes at the end of the Noonan section.)
3. The line where Red admits he has had sex with Dina on multiple occasions. (This part is early in the final section, just before the amber buttons comment.)
4. The bit where the zombie screams along with Monkey one night. (This is in the final section, an expansion of

Monkey screaming at night.)

Initially I compared the *Unintended Meetings* text to a Russian online text as well as a hardcopy text from the "Worlds of the Brothers Strugatsky" series (1997). Here is what I found:

With regard to the Russian Zone, the *Unintended Meetings* version is missing the five sentences. That paragraph also shows a word substitution and a sentence where the words are switched in order.

As for the zombie taking his drink, I was surprised to discover the *Unintended Meetings* edition includes this line.

On the topic of sex with Dina, the *Unintended Meetings* version lacks this half-sentence.

Regarding the zombie reply to Monkey's scream, the *Unintended Meetings* edition has this electrifying detail. There is a word cut, a word added, and a word substituted, though.

Thus the results are not uniform to my expectations. In fact, the text seems less censored than the Bouis translation. Granted, the *Unintended Meetings* text has sloppy mistakes, but it has elements the Bouis version lacks. The question arises as to the number of Russian editions compared with the two English translations.

Editions of *Roadside Picnic* in Russian and English
1972: serialized in a Russian magazine.
1973: (prologue and beginning of first part) published in the Russian book "Library of Modern Fiction."
1977: Bouis translation in English.
1980: *Unintended Meetings* version.
1984: published in Russian collection with "For a Billion Years Before the End of the World" (a separate novel known in English as *Definitely Maybe*).
1989: published in Russian book form by "Legal Literature" in two editions, one perhaps mistakenly a draft edition.

1991: published in Russian "White Edition."

1997: published in Russian as part of the omnibus series "Worlds of the Brothers Strugatsky" ("Mir Brat'ya Strugatsky").

2000: the above "Worlds of the Brothers Strugatsky" edition with some corrections, published as the "Black Collection" (2000 to 2003).

2012: Bormashenko translation in English.

•

I do not read Russian, so my comparison of Russian texts is purely pattern recognition, with aid from computer search and computer translation. In the course of comparing texts, I came to a realization about the online Russian/English side-by-side version (http://www.shnare sys.com/roadside/picnic/parallel.htm) that I was using as a tool: While the English text was cited as the Bouis translation, the Russian text did not match it, nor did the Russian text have any note on its source. Basically, my "Rosetta Stone" was not a Rosetta Stone at all; it was a misleading comparison of two different texts! (This caused a great deal of confusion: initially I was convinced that the text of the "Worlds of Brothers Strugatsky" edition [1996] was the same as the Bouis text [1977].)

Rebounding from this setback, I ended up with six different texts to compare with each other: the Russian online text (of unknown provenance), the Bouis translation (1977), the *Unintended Meetings* text (1980), the "Worlds of the Brothers Strugatsky" edition (1997), the Bormashenko translation (2012), and the Russian language Kindle edition (2015). They are presented in chronological order, except for the first Russian text.

Russian Text (online, side by side with Bouis translation)
0. BaPP: YES
1. Russian Zone: NO
2. Zombie Drink: YES
3. Dina Sex: NO
4. Zombie Cry: NO

Bouis English Translation (1977)
0. BaPP: term missing
1. Russian Zone: NO
2. Zombie Drink: NO
3. Dina Sex: NO
4. Zombie Cry: NO

Unintended Meetings **Anthology** (1980)
0. BaPP: as "BeeP;" Harmont as "Marmont"
1. Russian Zone: NO
2. Zombie Drink: YES
3. Dina Sex: NO
4. Zombie Cry: YES

Worlds of Brothers Strugatsky Edition (1997)
0. BaPP: YES
1. Russian Zone: YES
2. Zombie Drink: YES
3. Dina Sex: YES
4. Zombie Cry: YES

Bormashenko English Translation (2012)
0. BaPP: YES, as "Varr"
1. Russian Zone: YES
2. Zombie Drink: YES
3. Dina Sex: YES
4. Zombie Cry: YES

Kindle Edition, Russian, by Prospekt (2015)
0. BaPP: YES
1. Russian Zone: YES
2. Zombie Drink: YES
3. Dina Sex: YES
4. Zombie Cry: YES

The pattern suggests that by the time of the "Worlds of the Brothers Strugatsky" (1997) edition, the text of *Roadside Picnic* was largely restored, and further refinements presumably came in the editions of the "Black Collection" (2000–3).

It is probably true that the *Unintended Meetings* version is the worst for sloppy errors, but it appears that, as far as censorship goes, the Bouis English translation (1977) is the worst edition. This means that the two English editions have the curious quality of offering both the worst and the best.

****

Works Cited

Russian Wikipedia contributors. "Piknik na obochine." Russian Wikipedia.
<https://ru.wikipedia.org/wiki/Пикник_на_обочине>.
Accessed April 6, 2016.

Strugatsky, Arkady and Boris. *Roadside Picnic*, different editions as follows:
———. Russian online text (of unknown provenance).
<http://www.shnaresys.com/roadside/picnic/parallel.htm>. Accessed April 6, 2016.
———. Bouis English translation (1977).
<http://www.shnaresys.com/roadside/picnic/parallel.htm> Accessed April 6, 2016.
———. *Unintended Meetings* text ("Nenaznachennye Vstrechi"). Omnibus of "The Visitors," *Roadside Picnic,* and *Space Mowgli.* With illustrations. Moscow: Molodaya gvardiya, 1980.
———. "Worlds of the Brothers Strugatsky" edition ("Mir Brat'ya Strugatsky"). Omnibus of novels *Roadside Picnic, The*

Dead Mountaineer's Inn, and *Snail on a Slope*. Based on the 1996 text. With illustrations. Sankt-Peterburg: Terra Fantastika; Moscow: AST, 2004.

———. Bormashenko English translation. Chicago: Chicago Review Press, 2012.

———. Russian language Kindle edition. Prospekt, 2015.

REVIEW OF *THE DEAD MOUNTAINEER'S INN*

The Dead Mountaineer's Inn: One More Last Rite for the Detective Genre by Arkady and Boris Strugatsky (Brooklyn, New York: Melville House, 2015; $17.00 tpb; 256 pages)

The Brothers Strugatsky in 1970 penned this high-energy parody/homage regarding detective fiction: *The Dead Mountaineer's Inn.* It has finally been translated into English in 2015.

I enjoyed it a great deal. I did not know what it would be, and I do not want to ruin it for anybody, so I will tread carefully.

For starters, *The Dead Mountaineer's Inn* is nothing like their most famous work, *Roadside Picnic.* Instead it is a romp, a comedy that I found to be very amusing, and this is a side of the Brothers I had not seen before.

The detective himself tells the tale in first person, using an engaging tone that reminds me of Tsutsui's short stories. That is, it has an absurdist angle and a slipstream appearance in addition to balancing between mystery and anti-mystery. A juggling act, in short.

Here's the set up: our hero is on vacation at a remote

hotel in the mountains, when suddenly, out of nowhere, weird things begin to happen.

Sure, that sounds like a stereotypical start, and the tropes thereafter pile up faster than a snowdrift. But somehow it is all a lot of fun. Thrills! Chills! Spills!

There are ten quirky characters at the hotel, not counting the dog, Lel, a wonderful character himself. There is the owner, his one employee, and guests including a scientist, a hypnotist, a married couple, a youth counselor, a detective, and others.

Josh Billings translated it, and as far as I can tell he did a bang-up job. Jeff VanderMeer provides an introduction that reveals background details about the novel and the Brothers Strugatsky.

I'll have more to say about the novel, but that is enough for here and now!

ABOUT THE AUTHOR

Michael Andre-Driussi has written a number of science fiction reference books, from *Lexicon Urthus* (1994) to *Handbook of Vance Space* (2014). With Alice K. Turner he co-edited *Snake's-hands: the Fiction of John Crowley* (2001). His fiction, published in venues from *Aberrations* to *Wicked Words Quarterly*, has been collected in *Fallout Stories* (2016), *Doomsday and Other Tours* (2016), and *The Jizmatic Trilogy* (2017).